BURN AFTER WRITING

BURN AFTER WRITING

Sharon Jones

A TarcherPerigee Book

tarcherperigee

An imprint of Penguin Random House LLC
penguinrandomhouse.com

BURN AFTER WRITING

First American edition: August 2015
Originally published in Great Britain by Carpet Bombing Culture in 2014.

Most TarcherPerigee books are available at special quantity discounts for bulk purchases for sales
promotions, premiums, fund-raising, or educational use. Special books, or book excerpts, can also
be created to fit specific needs. For details, write: SpecialMarkets@penguinrandomhouse.com.

ISBN: 9780593543016

PRINTED IN THE UNITED STATES OF AMERICA

10 9 8 7 6 5 4 3 2 1

WELCOME TO THE BOOK OF YOU

As adults we learn to focus on representing ourselves in a manner pleasing to others. It's time to leave that behind you for a minute. Take some time out, grab a coffee, and indulge yourself with *Burn After Writing* by lamplight.

What is *Burn After Writing*?

It is your black dossier. Hidden in the secret compartment of your world. For your eyes only. The place where you speak your own truth freely, beyond any concern for how it might be viewed by others. The only space in your life where you can take off all the masks.

It's an extended feature-length interview with you, a radical thought experiment with you as the subject and you as the result.

Some elements are random, like tea leaves forming patterns in a mug. Some elements are more deliberate, to coax you into realizing things about yourself you never noticed before.

It's time to play a game of Truth or Dare with yourself. How honest can you really be with only yourself watching?

THE TRUTH

You can't hide from the truth, but it sure as hell can hide from you.

They say the artist is one who uses lies to tell the truth. One thing's for sure: It's impossible to tell the whole truth, especially when you are writing about yourself.

Sometimes the lie is in the omission. Sometimes the lie is in the spin. But there is always an element of fiction, because the talking or the writing is not the thing itself—the gap between the word and the moment is always too wide.

How honest can you be with these questions? How does it feel to tell the truth?

I suppose the real question here is this: How possible is it to see yourself clearly through your own supremely biased eyes?

However you choose to use this book, think about "the truth" before you answer.

At least then you might know if you're lying or not.

THE PEN IS MIGHTIER THAN THE KEYBOARD

Handwriting is like a fingerprint, a singing voice, a footstep: unique. Each person's handwriting style betrays as much in and of itself as in the intention with which it is used. You give yourself away when you take pen to paper.

In the age of infinite and instant reproduction only the unique is still beautiful. Will your descendants ever read your Facebook Timeline?

Save something for the real world, which remains, after all, the only place where we can really be ourselves. Write something beautiful by hand and you can be sure it will last for eternity.

DISCLAIMER

If you are not you, then you may not go further. For it is not written. You cannot simply skip in here without a care in the world and start prancing about the pages willy-nilly. No. You must be initiated into the cult of *BAW*.

Before you go on, like the fool about to step off a cliff, stop here a moment and consider the sacred values of the cult of *BAW*:

- I will answer with relentless, painfully searching honesty all questions within.

- I will use the power of the magical random "havaflickthru" to select the most relevant question for my present state.

- I will take a walk through the corridors of my mind and open all locked doors.

If you can commit to these noble and courageous values,

then by all means you are welcome to join the society of truth and self-knowledge. Copy out the following statement in your own handwriting:

I pledge my allegiance to the cult of *BAW*.

Now you may proceed. Keep the faith. And select a page at random. (Or is it selecting you . . . ?)

THE PAST

· · ·

You can't look at something without changing it;
you can't look at yourself without changing.

M aybe you can't change the past, but the way you
remember it is never the same twice. Every time we
remember something, we relive it from a different camera
angle.

We always reinvent our history to suit the present need.
Now let's do the opposite. Try to find new storylines in the
fragments of your own history, storylines that completely
re-create your relationship to the present. It's a fun game,
but there are lots of rules. Only you know what they are.
Proceed.

My earliest memory

As a child, I dreamed of becoming

When I look into the past, the thing I miss the most

My childhood described in one word

Posters I had on my wall growing up

.

The single most profound act of kindness that I will never forget

People in history I admire

MY FIRSTS

A first is like an earthquake of the soul. Unforgettable, unsustainable, and radically destructive. But out of the wreckage of our clumsy and passionate firsts comes a fabulously interesting and resilient adult individual. Our tragedy is that we always hope that the first time will last forever.

First friend: ....

First love: ....

First record/CD bought: ....

First foreign holiday: ....

First job: ....

First car: ....

First concert: ....

First school: ....

First kiss: ....

First teacher: ....

First alcoholic drink: ....

When was the last time you did something for the first time?

LOOKING BACK

Take a walk through the garden of memory into the hazy half-remembered days of your personal history. Everybody's talking about the good old days . . .

The music I loved as a child

The first thing I bought with my own money

The age at which I became an adult

The person who had the greatest impact on my life

The person I have loved the most

The hardest thing I've ever done

If I could do it all over again, I would change

The first song I ever remember hearing

Things I collected as a child

My aspirations as a child

The teacher that had the most influence on my life

My parents were

My first pet

My best friend growing up

The long-lost childhood possession that I would love to see again

The one thing I regret in the whole world

.

Things that I have been addicted to

I was most happy when

The book that has had the greatest influence on my life

The most dramatic fork in the road in my life

I will never forgive

The craziest thing I have ever done in my life

5 things I am glad I tried but will never do again

1. ....

2. ....

3. ....

4. ....

5. ....

The 5 best times I've ever had in my life

1. ....

2. ....

3. ....

4. ....

5. ....

5 things that I have always wanted to do but have never done

1. ....

2. ....

3. ....

4. ....

5. ....

People I miss

I wish I had never met

The last time I said "I love you"

My greatest heartbreak

The smartest choice I made as a teenager

I feel guilty for

My life story in 3 sentences

Baggage I am carrying

A FEW OF MY FAVORITE THINGS

Every now and then something comes along that knocks you off your feet. You feel like you have finally been understood, like somebody looked into your soul and wrote a song just for you. And as you grow, these things grow with you, making your life richer.

Top 5 bands

1. ....

2. ....

3. ....

4. ....

5. ....

Top 5 albums

1. ....

2. ....

3. ....

4. ....

5. ....

Top 5 songs

1. ....

2. ....

3. ....

4. ....

5. ....

Top 5 concerts

1. ....

2. ....

3. ....

4. ....

5. ....

Top 5 books

1. ....

2. ....

3. ....

4. ....

5. ....

Top 5 movies

1. ....

2. ....

3. ....

4. ....

5. ....

Top 5 places in the world

1. ....

2. ....

3. ....

4. ....

5. ....

Top 5 cities

1. ....

2. ....

3. ....

4. ....

5. ....

Top 5 most amazing experiences

1. ....

2. ....

3. ....

4. ....

5. ....

Top 5 "regular" people

1. ....

2. ....

3. ....

4. ....

5. ....

Top 5 celebrities

1. ....

2. ....

3. ....

4. ....

5. ....

Top 5 creative geniuses

1. ....

2. ....

3. ....

4. ....

5. ....

If I could spend 48 hours with anyone (living or dead), it would be

If I could have lived through any time period, it would have been

The last 3 years of my life described in 3 words

1. ....

2. ....

3. ....

5 milestone experiences that made me the person that I am today

1. ....

2. ....

3. ....

4. ....

5. ....

The hardest choice I have ever had to make

The stupidest thing I have ever done

How cool would my 16-year-old self think I am right now?

My favorite childhood memory

QUICK FIRE

I've

- [ ] Been in love
- [ ] Failed my driving test
- [ ] Jumped out of a plane
- [ ] Broken a bone
- [ ] Won a trophy
- [ ] Learned another language
- [ ] Been to a spa
- [ ] Kissed someone and regretted it
- [ ] Smoked a cigar
- [ ] Ridden in an ambulance
- [ ] Turned someone down
- [ ] Flown in a helicopter
- [ ] Met someone famous
- [ ] Written my will
- [ ] Read my partner's Internet history
- [ ] Learned the words to the national anthem
- [ ] Been a godparent
- [ ] Buried someone
- [ ] Gotten married
- [ ] Showered with someone else
- [ ] Given blood
- [ ] Memorized a poem
- [ ] Broken something expensive
- [ ] Considered cosmetic surgery
- [ ] Bungee jumped
- [ ] Had cosmetic surgery
- [ ] Danced with my mother/father
- [ ] Jumped off the high board
- [ ] Dived off the high board
- [ ] Been on a diet
- [ ] Had an invisible friend
- [ ] Been a best man/bridesmaid
- [ ] Dated someone twice
- [ ] Won a competition
- [ ] Deleted my Internet history
- [ ] Made a speech in front of an audience
- [ ] Cheated on someone

QUICK FIRE

I've

- ☐ Stayed out all night
- ☐ Been on a blind date
- ☐ Had a massage
- ☐ Sung karaoke
- ☐ Watched the sun rise
- ☐ Watched the sun set
- ☐ Lost at a casino
- ☐ Faked it
- ☐ Grown my own food
- ☐ Changed a car tire
- ☐ Kissed a stranger
- ☐ Been on TV
- ☐ Given money to a panhandler
- ☐ Gotten divorced
- ☐ Handwritten a love letter
- ☐ Climbed a mountain
- ☐ Been on a diet twice
- ☐ Sent a message in a bottle
- ☐ Told at least one good joke
- ☐ Worked for minimum wage
- ☐ Won a bet

- ☐ Written poetry
- ☐ Performed on stage
- ☐ Fired a gun
- ☐ Been to a school reunion
- ☐ DJed
- ☐ Ridden a mechanical bull
- ☐ Learned first aid
- ☐ Saved someone's life
- ☐ Broken someone's heart
- ☐ Volunteered for charity
- ☐ Lied to a police officer
- ☐ Learned a card trick
- ☐ Gotten a degree
- ☐ Had a pen pal
- ☐ Stayed up for 24 hours straight
- ☐ Sponsored a child
- ☐ Done a split
- ☐ Lied to the doctor
- ☐ Gotten married again
- ☐ Signed up as an organ donor
- ☐ Had a tarot card reading

THINGS THAT I HAVE LEARNED
ALONG THE WAY . . .

I CONFESS

Nothing lightens the soul quite like a good hearty confession. Let this page act as your confessional box.

At some point in my childhood, my friends and I went outside to play together for the very last time, and none of us knew it.*

If I could go back, this is who would be there

And this is where we'd be

---
* internet anonymous

FIRSTS AND LASTS

A first is momentous. It's both meaningful and memorable. Crammed with new possibilities and the excitement of whatever comes next. But give a little thought for the last times too. Chock full of consequence and aftermath. Endings that at the time you didn't even see coming . . .

The first word I would use to describe myself: ....

The last time I felt happy: ....

The first thing I would do if I were in charge of the country: ....

The last thing I think of before I go to sleep: ....

My first love: ....

The last time I cried: ....

The first person I would confide in: ....

The last person I would rely on: ....

The first time I had my heart broken: ....

The last time I said I love you: ....

The first quality I look for in a person: ....

The last time I felt in control: ....

The first time I stood my ground: ....

The last time I faked it: ....

The first person I would call in a crisis: ....

The last time I congratulated myself: ....

My first real relationship: ....

The last time I set my heart on something: ....

The first time I lost a loved one: ....

The last time I failed at something: ....

The first time I thought I'd made it: ....

The last time I felt a success: ....

The first song that moved me: ....

The last time I said thank you: ....

The first person I had a crush on: ....

The last time I was angry: ....

The first thing I would save in a house fire: ....

The last time I gave it 100 percent: ....

The first time I felt time was running out: ....

The last time I was fearful: ....

The first time I felt like an adult: ....

The last time I did something for the first time: ....

And last but not least . . .
The last time I lied? ....

Three things I forgive myself for

Three signs of hope for the future

Three things my alter ego would do differently

THE PRESENT

· · ·

YOLO (You Only Live Once)

This is the same moment in which all of history occurred. Everything is contained within it. Nothing lies without.

Everybody wants you to live for the moment. Primarily because it is easier to sell things to a goldfish with ADHD. But where are you actually right now? To answer that you have to step outside the present moment into a space of reflection.

You have to stop time, get off the ride, and look back on it. The only way to really see the present is to be outside of it. So put yourself into words. Freeze your restless subjectivity into a crystallized state, like crushing a butterfly inside a scrapbook.

See through the chaotic circus of the lived moment to the gems of relevant truth beyond.

Where are you? Right now?

Who are you right now?

The biggest inspiration in my life

My most prized possession

Today I learned

Things I should let go of

If I was given $10,000, I would spend it on

The one song that makes the hairs on the back of my neck stand up

3 things that are getting on my nerves right now

1. ....

2. ....

3. ....

If a genie granted me 3 wishes, they would be

1. ....

2. ....

3. ....

The first 5 songs that play when I press "shuffle" on my media player

1. ....

2. ....

3. ....

4. ....

5. ....

The one thing I want to change about myself

If I could have a conversation today with one person from history, it would be

My life quote

The one relationship I would like to fix

Things that make me happy

My autobiography would be called

My favorite "little things" in life

If I could give one thing to one person it would be

Things that make me laugh

I secretly envy

If I could be anywhere in the world right now

If I could be a fly on the wall

My greatest fear

47

THIS IS WHO I AM

Live for the now or plan for the future? Everybody seems to have their own idea.

Listen. Don't listen. Be where you are. Be who you are.

Everybody tells you these are the best days of your life. So much pressure! They're all wrong. Be where you are. Nobody else is really having any more fun than you are. They're all just pretending.

The thing that I am working on that is BIG

My personality in 6 words

1. ....

2. ....

3. ....

4. ....

5. ....

6. ....

If I didn't know how old I was, I would think I was

If I could choose to stay a certain age forever, it would be

If I could go to the fridge right now and find one thing

5 things I need in my life

1. ....

2. ....

3. ....

4. ....

5. ....

5 things I want in my life

1. ....

2. ....

3. ....

4. ....

5. ....

LET'S BE HONEST

Let's pretend there is something under the mask. Is there?
Who are you?

I am: ....

I'm not: ....

I adore: ....

I detest: ....

I have: ....

I have never: ....

I like: ....

I don't like: ....

I love: ....

I hate: ....

I need: ....

I want: ....

I can: ....

I can't: ....

I'm always: ....

I'm never: ....

I'm afraid of: ....

I'm not afraid to: ....

I'm pretty good at: ....

I'm no good at: ....

I want more: ....

I want less: ....

I can never respect

If I could change my first name, I would change it to

If I had to be trapped in a TV show, it would be

If I could lock one person in a room and torment them for a day, that person would be

The one thing I don't mind spending a lot of money on

If I had a brainwashing machine, I would use it on

The first song to come into my head right now is

If I were to win the lottery, this amount would be enough

If I could pick up the phone right now and call one person, living or
dead, it would be

I AM

Circle one of the two characteristics on each line that you feel best describes your personality.

Anxious   OR   Calm

Stubborn   OR   Flexible

Daring   OR   Cautious

Moody   OR   Cheerful

See Big Picture   OR   Detail Oriented

Competitive   OR   Cooperative

Pessimistic   OR   Optimistic

Patient   OR   Hasty

Suspicious   OR   Trusting

THE LAST WORD

Fleeting moments fly past us, whistling in the wind. Can you catch one out of the air like Mr. Miyagi catching flies with chopsticks in *The Karate Kid* (the original, not the remake)?

Last film:

Last book:

Last concert:

Last time I cried:

Last song I listened to:

Last time I was scared:

Last time I danced:

Last time I was angry:

Last time I laughed:

Last time I was drunk:

I need to forgive

If I could clean up one mess, it would be

The one skill I wish I could possess

If I was exiled to a foreign land for the rest of my life, I would like it to be

My foolproof recipe for mending a broken heart

If I had to sacrifice one of my relatives to save the world, it would be

The 3 finest meals I have ever produced by my own hand

1. ....

2. ....

3. ....

If my house was on fire, the 3 things I would grab are

1. ....

2. ....

3. ....

ONE WORD

Think fast. Better still, don't think at all. Sidestep your own mental filters and cut to the chase. Don't pause, don't ponder, and don't criticize. If you could say everything you wanted with just one word . . .

My job: ....

My partner: ....

My body: ....

My love life: ....

My sanctuary: ....

My fear: ....

My childhood: ....

My addiction: ....

My passion: ....

My kryptonite: ....

My regret: ....

ONE WORD

My turn-on: ....

My turn-off: ....

My hero: ....

My future: ....

My fantasy: ....

My Achilles' heel: ....

My guilt: ....

My greatest virtue: ....

My vice: ....

The outcome is bigger than the sum of its parts

.... + ... + ... = Family

.... + ... + ... = Love

.... + ... + ... = Life

Looking at the lives of my friends, this is who I think has gotten it right

If I could install 3 complete languages in my brain (with zero effort),
I would choose

If I could bring one person back from the dead right now, it would be

The single biggest waste of energy in my life right now

People I'd like to punch in the face

If I could go back in time and witness any historical event, it would be

The things that are taboo for me, the things I find hard to talk about even with close friends

People to be forgiven

The things I find ridiculous

PEOPLE THAT MEAN SOMETHING TO ME

If I could make one thing vanish forever, it would be

My parents in 5 words

1. ....

2. ....

3. ....

4. ....

5. ....

The biggest hole in my life was left by

If I was given $10,000 today on the condition that I couldn't keep
the money for myself, I would

Right now, at this moment, the thing I want the most is

The one word I would use to describe the relationship with my mother

The one word I would use to describe the relationship with my father

The advice that has shaped me the most

If I could direct the Hollywood movie of my life story, it would be called

And this would be the cast list:

.... **as** me ....

.... **as** ....

.... **as** ....

.... **as** ....

.... **as** ....

.... **as** ....

.... **as** ....

.... **as** ....

.... **as** ....

The song for the opening credits of the movie of my life

The song for the main theme of the movie of my life

The song for the closing credits of the movie of my life

Religion in 3 words

1. ....

2. ....

3. ....

One word to describe my current love life

If I had to sing one karaoke tune in a crowded bar of strangers, my song would be

If I were to host a dinner party and I could invite 3 people (dead or alive) as fellow diners, they would be

The full names of my children today (born or otherwise)

SOMETHING THAT MEANS SOMETHING

MY ATTRIBUTES

Be honest. You judge everybody you meet. We all do.

How about judging yourself for a change?

Honesty	1	2	3	4	5	6	7	8	9	10
Generosity	1	2	3	4	5	6	7	8	9	10
Forgiveness	1	2	3	4	5	6	7	8	9	10
Happiness	1	2	3	4	5	6	7	8	9	10
Loyalty	1	2	3	4	5	6	7	8	9	10
Uniqueness	1	2	3	4	5	6	7	8	9	10
Humor	1	2	3	4	5	6	7	8	9	10
Intelligence	1	2	3	4	5	6	7	8	9	10
Accommodating	1	2	3	4	5	6	7	8	9	10
Talented	1	2	3	4	5	6	7	8	9	10
Confidence	1	2	3	4	5	6	7	8	9	10
Humbleness	1	2	3	4	5	6	7	8	9	10
Loving	1	2	3	4	5	6	7	8	9	10
Tolerance	1	2	3	4	5	6	7	8	9	10
Spontaneity	1	2	3	4	5	6	7	8	9	10
Health	1	2	3	4	5	6	7	8	9	10
Creativity	1	2	3	4	5	6	7	8	9	10
Fashionable	1	2	3	4	5	6	7	8	9	10

I am sick to death of hearing about

If no one was watching, I would

The most valuable thing I own is

My guiltiest pleasure

If I could make one thing disappear today, it would be

My secret skill

The song title that best describes my life

If I had two weeks to live, I would

The one thing that I do that I would like to be able to stop

If I could change one current event in the world, it would be

I'm worried about

My darkest secret

WORD ASSOCIATION

When I say "life," you say what? Don't think; just write the first word that comes into your head. Let your subconscious mind do the talking. You might be surprised at what you discover about yourself through the magical power of randomness.

Life: ....

Past: ....

Work: ....

Sex: ....

Trust: ....

Excess: ....

Fame: ....

Hate: ....

Forgiveness: ....

Innocence: ....

Weakness: ....

Victim: ....

Death: ....

Violence: ....

Discipline: ....

Regret: ....

Lies: ....

Mother: ....

Sadness: ....

Religion: ....

Domination: ....   Fear: ....

Love: ....   Home: ....

Family: ....   Drugs: ....

Sacrifice: ....   Future: ....

Age: ....   Failure: ....

Honesty: ....   Destiny: ....

War: ....   Humor: ....

Success: ....   Envy: ....

Lust: ....   Honesty: ....

5 things I love to hate

1. ....

2. ....

3. ....

4. ....

5. ....

The nicest thing I've ever done that no one knows about

At the end of the day, who will be there for me?

On a scale of 1 to 10, how happy am I with my life?

1   2   3   4   5   6   7   8   9   10

What would make it a 10?

MY LIFE IN TRIVIA

Birthplace: ....

Siblings: ....

Currently residing: ....

Social class: ....

Occupation: ....

Zodiac sign: ....

Political party: ....

Allergy: ....

Pet: ....

Charity: ....

Newspaper: ....

Magazine: ....

Drink: ....

Breakfast: ....

Starter: ....

Main course: ....

Dessert: ....

Restaurant: ....

Bar: ....

Club: ....

Hotel: ....

Clothing: ....

Shoes: ....

Car: ....

Phone: ....

Camera: ....

Dream job: ....

Subscription: ....

Computer: ....

Brand: ....

Shop: ....

Comfort food: ....

Hobby: ....

Pastime: ....

Team: ....

Game: ....

Website: ....

TV program: ....

FAMILY IS

How in control of my life do I feel right now?

1   2   3   4   5   6   7   8   9   10

What would make it a 10?

My dream job

My favorite food

My most treasured possession

My perfect Saturday night

Something I've wished for repeatedly

My hidden talent

The things that I am really bad at

The one movie that I could watch over and over again

ALL-TIME FAVORITES

Song: ....

Album: ....

Concert: ....

Place: ....

Movie: ....

Book: ....

Band: ....

Artist: ....

Holiday: ....

City: ....

Teacher: ....

Word: ....

TV program: ....

PRICELESS

The things that money can't buy

WALK ON THE WILD SIDE

Sometimes the right thing to do is the wrong thing. Sensible people are basically idiots. We're not sure how that adds up, but it does. The world is wrong, so how can doing wrong in the eyes of the world possibly be wrong?

Things I've Done

- ☐ Been skinny dipping
- ☐ Been in a police car
- ☐ Taken drugs
- ☐ Been drunk
- ☐ Been in a fight
- ☐ Seen someone/something die
- ☐ Partied all night
- ☐ Smoked cigarettes
- ☐ Been fired from a job
- ☐ Had stitches
- ☐ Gotten a tattoo
- ☐ Faked it
- ☐ Crashed a party
- ☐ Cheated on a test
- ☐ Danced in the moonlight
- ☐ Skipped a class
- ☐ Stolen something
- ☐ Been to a music festival
- ☐ Joined the mile-high club

- ☐ Gotten a piercing
- ☐ Dyed my hair
- ☐ Kissed a stranger
- ☐ Had a friend with benefits
- ☐ Had my heart broken
- ☐ Gone commando
- ☐ Eaten something that's alive
- ☐ Had sex outdoors
- ☐ Had cosmetic surgery
- ☐ Been thrown out of a club
- ☐ Protested against something
- ☐ Cheated on someone
- ☐ Fired a gun
- ☐ Taken revenge
- ☐ Smoked a cigar
- ☐ Broken the speed limit
- ☐ Drank champagne straight out of the bottle
- ☐ Played cards for money
- ☐ Fallen in love with someone I shouldn't have
- ☐ Bought porn
- ☐ Cross-dressed
- ☐ Been to a strip club
- ☐ Shoplifted
- ☐ Prank called someone
- ☐ Skipped work

The 3 people in the world that I'm most close to
(described in 3 words)

---

1. ....

2. ....

3. ....

---

1. ....

2. ....

3. ....

---

1. ....

2. ....

3. ....

The 5 people that I would like to thank (just for being themselves)

1. ....

2. ....

3. ....

4. ....

5. ....

MY MANTRAS FOR LIVING . . . AND MY RULES FOR LIFE

A LETTER TO MY FORMER SELF

THE FUTURE

. . .

Where am I going?

Predicting your future requires an element of self-delusion. The difficulty is that sometimes we can make something happen as we intend to and sometimes we cannot. And even when the intention is clear, the consequences must always be largely unforeseen. Fortunately, our intention is rarely very clear.

Where are you going? Where are you going? Where are you going? But really, where are you going though? How about now? And now? And be clear on this: The question is not where do you want to go or even where do you fancifully dream you will end up. Look at what you actually do. Look at the patterns in the rhythm of your everyday life and extrapolate accordingly. Remember to take this section very seriously because then it will be much funnier when you come back to read it in ten years' time.

And with our course set for the straits of foolhardy prediction, let us begin . . .

My future in 3 words

1. ....

2. ....

3. ....

3 things I need to let go of

1. ....

2. ....

3. ....

I DREAM OF

The one thing I'm most excited about

The one thing I'm most concerned about

My ideal home

The risk I would take if I knew I could not fail

The one thing that I would be prepared to die for

I must make room for

? OR ?

This beats the Myers-Briggs personality profiling matrix any day of the week. Remember: It's not what you're like that counts in this shallow world . . . it's what you like.

The Ride	OR	the Destination
The Stones	OR	the Beatles
Mac	OR	PC
Wine	OR	Spirits
Rich	OR	Famous
BMW	OR	Mercedes
Sweet	OR	Salted
Meat	OR	Murder
God	OR	the Big Bang
Pepsi	OR	Coke
London	OR	New York
Nike	OR	Adidas
Tea	OR	Coffee
Gay	OR	Straight
Movies	OR	Music
Summer	OR	Winter
Political Left	OR	Right
Truth	OR	Dare
Spirituality	OR	Religion
Climate Change Fact	OR	Fiction
City	OR	Country
Death Penalty	OR	Life Imprisonment
Hitchcock	OR	Spielberg
See the Future	OR	Change the Past

Las Vegas	OR	Paris
Art	OR	Science
Fame	OR	Money
Brains	OR	Beauty
Going Out	OR	Staying In
iPhone	OR	Droid
More Time	OR	More Money
Subway	OR	McDonald's
Watch the Movie	OR	Read the Book
Lennon	OR	McCartney
Freedom	OR	Security
Mountains	OR	Beach
Creativity	OR	Knowledge
Tattoos	OR	Piercings
The Wire	OR	*The Sopranos*
Money	OR	Looks
Odd	OR	Even
Appetizer	OR	Dessert
Adventure	OR	Relaxation
Telephone	OR	Text
Celebrity	OR	Artist
Cremation	OR	Burial
Winning Is Everything	OR	It's Taking Part That Matters
How Things Work	OR	How Things Look
Form	OR	Function
Thoughts	OR	Emotions
Slow	OR	Fast
Optimist	OR	Pessimist
Realist	OR	Idealist
Head	OR	Heart

. . . or neither

Something I think everyone should experience in their lifetime

The greatest enemy of the future of mankind

My dream reunion

If I could go on a trip right now, it would be to

The victory I am working toward

My next challenge

The 3 things that I have been putting off that I need to do

The one thing I'll do with my children differently than my parents did with me

The biggest challenge facing the world today

THE FUTURE IS

Let's play the predictions game! What do you want from the future?

10 places to go before I die

1. ....

2. ....

3. ....

4. ....

5. ....

6. ....

7. ....

8. ....

9. ....

10. ....

10 books I want to read

1. ....

2. ....

3. ....

4. ....

5. ....

6. ....

7. ....

8. ....

9. ....

10. ....

MY FAVORITE LYRICS/POETRY

In ten years' time, my money is coming from

I would like to retire to

My perfect road trip

The things that scare me about getting old

If I could spend my last hours of life with anyone, doing anything, I would

If I could be laid to rest anywhere, I would like it to be

The one song that I would like to be played at my funeral

MY LEGACY IS

PLAYLIST

These songs are the soundtrack to my life:

1. ....

2. ....

3. ....

4. ....

5. ....

6. ....

7. ....

8. ....

9. ....

10. ....

VOW—NOW

Circle your pledges. Add your own!

Say no

Forgive myself for my mistakes

Have no regrets

Prioritize

Sleep more

Treat myself

Shake things up

Give more

Fall in love

Take responsibility

Accept criticism

Make art

Be me

Work smarter, not harder

Worry less

Help others

Love more

Embrace change

Listen more

Don't hate

Take chances

Tell the truth

Be assertive

Be more humble

Relax more

Apologize

Lighten up

Eat good food

Smile more

Travel more

Dream big

Feel good anyway

Give credit, take blame

Be thankful

THE FUTURE STARTS HERE

One week from now, I will

One month from now, I will

One year from now, I will

Ten years from now, I will

MY LIFE RULES

#1

#2

#3

#4

#5

THE BUCKET LIST

Nothing lasts forever, least of all you. Let a little contemplation on mortality rev up your engines and reboot your lust for life. Old Death may be coming on his bony horse, but you won't go softly into that good night. Give yourself something good to flash before your eyes in the ultimate moment.

Cross things off this list and then start your own.

Run a half marathon

Do a triathlon

Ski/snowboard

Canoe

Ride a horse

Learn a new language

Play a musical instrument

Sing in a choir

Dance salsa

Ride in a hot air balloon

Jump out of a plane

Scuba dive

White water raft

Play chess

Make pottery

Paint a picture

Write a short story

Solve a Rubik's Cube

Volunteer/fund-raise

Start my own business

Ride a motorbike

Write a book

Donate blood

Bungee jump

Go camping

Climb a mountain

Plant a tree

Fly in a helicopter

Fire a gun

Go backpacking

Give to charity

Go rock climbing

Learn to juggle

Write my will

Milk a cow

Be part of a flash mob

Learn a martial art

Learn first aid

Learn to fly

Get a tattoo

Start a blog

Join a gym

Bake a cake

Find my "thing"

Learn to meditate

Go on a road trip

Try yoga

Learn to knit

Be happy

10 things to do before I die

1. ....

2. ....

3. ....

4. ....

5. ....

6. ....

7. ....

8. ....

9. ....

10. ....

I WANT LESS

I WANT MORE

LIFE IS

Freedom is being able to make your own definitions.

Life is: ....

Regret is: ....

Success is: ....

Children are: ....

Death is: ....

Happiness is: ....

Love is: ....

Faith is: ....

Work is: ....

Money is: ....

Peace is: ....

Religion is: ....

Politics is: ....

STUFF I WANT TO PASS ON

Imagine you have 9 minutes to live and you have a pen and paper. You can get a message to your children or someone close to you, giving them the best that you have learned. Give them something to carry with them in their own lives. What do you have to pass on? Go!

LOVE IS

MY INSPIRATION

MY PARTNER

Take a moment to consider your other half, whether it be current, future, or even past. It's an opportunity to look for the good, the bad, and the ugly of just why he or she is "the one."

The future is: ....

Our special moment: ....

Our song: ....

Our city: ....

5 things I love about you

1. ....

2. ....

3. ....

4. ....

5. ....

My turn-ons: ....

My turn-offs: ....

One thing I'd change about you: ....

My confession: ....

5 things you do that drive me crazy

1. ....

2. ....

3. ....

4. ....

5. ....

My perfect date night

Where it all started

What I love about you

I'll love you more if —

THEY ARE

Circle one of the two characteristics on each line that you feel best describes your partner's personality.

Anxious	OR	Calm
Stubborn	OR	Flexible
Daring	OR	Cautious
Moody	OR	Cheerful
See Big Picture	OR	Detail Oriented
Competitive	OR	Cooperative
Pessimistic	OR	Optimistic
Patient	OR	Hasty
Suspicious	OR	Trusting

LOVE IS THE ANSWER

I would love to learn: ....

I would love to go to: ....

I would love to try: ....

I would love to make: ....

I would love to let go of: ....

I would love to study: ....

I would love to talk to: ....

I would love to see: ....

I would love to learn to: ....

I would love to change: ....

I would love to help: ....

I would love to stop: ....

I would love to be: ....

HELLO, THIS IS THE FUTURE CALLING . . .

In 10 years' time I will . . .

Be driving a: ....

Be focused on: ....

Be celebrating: ....

Be living in: ....

Be working as: ....

Be interested in: ....

Be needing a: ....

Be learning: ....

Be a successful: ....

Be serious about: ....

Be having fun with: ....

Be on the path to: ....

Be still in touch with: ....

Be trying to find: ....

Be happy to have left: ....

Be mastering: ....

Be trying to change: ....

Be laughing at: ....

Be thankful for: ....

Be missing: ....

Be traveling to: ....

A TEXT I'LL NEVER SEND

A MEMORY I'LL NEVER SHARE

A LETTER I'D LOVE TO SEND

A LETTER I'D LOVE TO RECEIVE

WHY?

WHY NOT?

A LETTER TO MY FUTURE SELF

MY PLANS FOR THE FUTURE

THE TIME CAPSULE

Repeat after me . . .

I will not . . . mindlessly follow orders.

Now forget that and do as I tell you. Because I am you. I am the voice inside your head.

Pick a number between 1 and 10. Peel an orange and throw it over your shoulder. Roll some dice. Make an actual decision.

You will come back to this book when a number of years have passed and do all the exercises again.

Then you can meet yourself, like in that weird dream you keep having, only you're considerably more interesting now.

Congratulations, truth seeker. You reached the end of the vision quest. You know yourself a little better, for better or for worse. And maybe you realized that your "self" is just a construct, a thing you make and remake every day.

Or maybe not.

Or maybe.

BURN AFTER
WRITING?